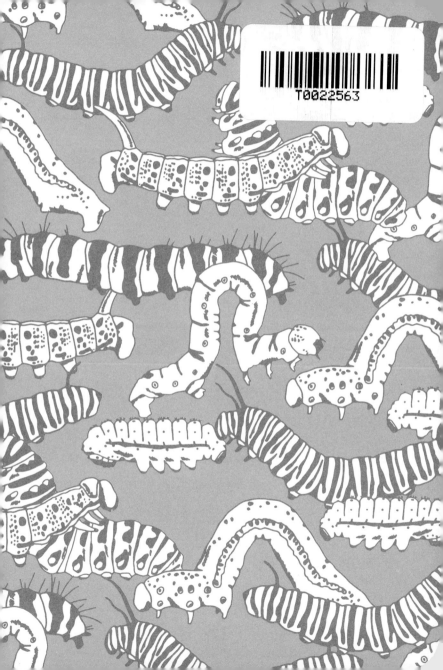

A Kid's Guide to
BACKYARD BUGS

Eliza Berkowitz

illustrated by
Nicole LaRue

Gibbs Smith

INTRODUCTION

Did you know that some types of scorpions can live for a year without food? Or that there's an earthworm that grows to be 6 feet long? You probably already know about ladybugs, but do you know about wheelbugs? How about the woolly bear (which is not a bear at all!)? You may have spent years learning about creepy, crawly bugs, or you may just be getting started. Either way, there's lots to learn. Bugs are fascinating!

Every time you step outside, there are opportunities to spot bugs. If you help care for a garden, you will likely come face-to-face with some creepy crawlies. If you grow fruits or vegetables, you will also likely spot some interesting insects. What about trips to the beach, park, or playground? Bugs are everywhere! When you take the time to look for them, you'll be surprised by how many you cross paths with every day.

This book will get you familiar with the 40 bugs you're most likely to see in the United States. Some of these bugs are much more common than others. You'll learn what they eat, what their life cycle looks like, and so much more. At the back of the book, there's a bug log to help you keep track of all the bugs you have spotted. How many of the bugs in this book can you find?

Learning about bugs is fun for people of all ages. And it's something the whole family can do together. You don't need anything special to get started, just an appreciation for the many types of crawling, flying, wiggling creatures found in nature.

DIY PROJECT

Want to create a safe place for bugs, from which you can observe and appreciate their weird ways? You can create your very own bug hotel! Providing some shelter for insects can be a fun project for you, but also great for the bugs too. To get started, gather some of the materials below.

PINE CONES

LEAVES

STICKS AND TWIGS

Next, find the perfect place to build your structure. Look for a spot that's not too sunny or dry. (Many bugs prefer damp, dark areas.) Then, use your imagination and start to piece your palace together. Maybe it looks like a tent with sticks forming the outside and filled with bark and leaves. Or perhaps it looks like a nest with pine cones, rocks, and twigs creating the perfect hiding spots. Think about ways to use logs to form a happy hideaway. There's no right or wrong way to create a bug hotel. It can be as big or as small as you like!

LOG (OLDER, ROTTING LOGS ARE BEST!)

BARK

STONES AND ROCKS

BRICKS

IDENTIFICATION

Most bugs share a similar bodily structure. This is composed of three segments: the **head**, **thorax**, and **abdomen**. They do not have a skeleton, but they do have an **exoskeleton**. This is a hard shell covering the outside of its body.

A bug's **eyes** help with sight. The **antennae** are used for smell or to help feel what's around. The **mouthparts** are used for chewing and eating. These are all parts of the **head**.

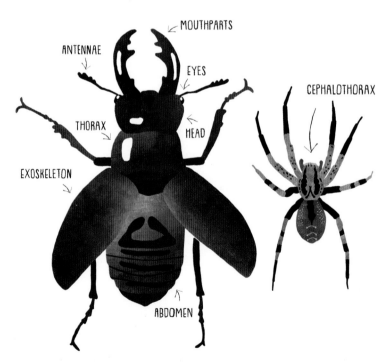

MOUTHPARTS

ANTENNAE

EYES

CEPHALOTHORAX

THORAX

HEAD

EXOSKELETON

ABDOMEN

The **thorax** is the middle section. This is where the legs and wings attach to the body. Most bugs have three sets of legs and two sets of wings.

The **abdomen** is the rear section. This contains the stomach and other organs that help with digestion and reproduction.

Spiders have a slightly different bodily structure. They have a **cephalothorax**. This is a single part that contains the head and thorax. Spiders usually have four sets of legs, no wings, and no antennae.

Here are a few terms that will help you understand a bug's life cycle:

The **egg** is usually the first stage of an insect's life. Eggs are laid by a female, sometimes in clusters or groups.

A **larva** hatches from an egg. Larvae often look like tiny worms.

Before a larva can become an adult, it will go through a process where it changes form completely. This is called **metamorphosis**.

A **pupa** is a cocoon a young insect forms around itself as it goes through metamorphosis. When it emerges from the pupa, it is now an adult insect.

A **nymph** is a young insect. Some insects are born looking like small versions of an adult. These insects don't have a larval stage. They don't form pupae and they don't undergo metamorphosis. Instead, they **molt**. This is the process of shedding skin as they grow. Some bugs molt many times.

WHAT'S IN MY BAG?

The next time you're looking for a fun activity, consider going on a bug hunt! Lace up your sneakers, step outside, and head to an area with trees, plants, or flowers. Don't forget that many bugs like to stay hidden. Picking up stones, digging in dirt, and looking under logs are good places to start. You don't need any special supplies, but here are a few things that would be helpful to have:

A **magnifying glass** can help you get a close-up look at smaller bugs. It will help you see details that you might have missed.

Some **empty jars** can come in handy, if you want to trap a bug so you can study it. A **small net** can help with this too. It's better not to touch any bugs that are not familiar. Remember to treat any bugs you capture with care. And put them back where you found them!

A **camera** is nice to have. When you've taken photos, you can go back and zoom in to see any details you missed. Or you may just want to save them as a reminder of the bugs you've seen!

Sneakers or **hiking boots** will keep your feet comfy if you're doing a lot of walking. When you're traveling on uneven ground, like in a wooded area, proper footwear can also prevent injuries.

Keep a **notebook** and **pen** handy. You never know when you might see an unusual bug and want to jot down its features or behaviors.

And finally, don't forget **this book** to help you identify the bugs you come across!

SIZE

About 2½ inches long.
That's half the length of a
dollar bill.

SCORPION

order Scorpiones

Good news about scorpions: They rarely attack humans. Bad news about scorpions: Most are **venomous**. That means they inject a poison when they sting. This could lead to sickness or even death. A scorpion's stinger is located at the end of its long, curved tail. At the front of its body, they have a pair of **pincers**. These help them catch **prey**, defend themselves, and dig burrows. Scorpions can vary in size, shape, and coloring. Those that live in deserts are usually yellowish or light brown. Scorpions in the mountains or in moist climates are usually brown or black.

FOOD

Scorpions will eat any small animal they can capture. This includes insects, spiders, small rodents, lizards, and even other scorpions!

LIFE CYCLE

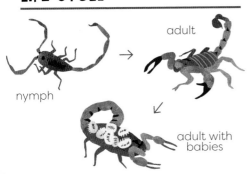

nymph

adult

adult with babies

■ **YEAR-ROUND**

HABITAT & RANGE

The most common **habitat** for scorpions is the hot, dry desert, but they have gotten used to other climates too. Most scorpions in the United States live in Arizona, California, and New Mexico.

BUG ABODE

Scorpions are **nocturnal**. They hide in holes, cracks, and under rocks during the day. At night, they come out to look for food.

FUN FACTS

The longest scorpion is South Africa's rock scorpion. Females can grow to be almost 8½ inches long!

Some types of scorpions can live without food for up to a year.

11

SIZE

About 3 inches long.
That's as long as three
paperclips.

PRAYING MANTIS

Mantis religiosa

Have you ever seen a praying mantis? If so, count yourself lucky! These insects are hard to spot. They can **camouflage** or blend into their surroundings. They are most likely to be seen in leafy or woody areas where their brown or green color blends in. They have a triangular head and big eyes. Although not very long, they are fierce **predators**. It's not uncommon for a praying mantis to go after **prey** three times its size!

FOOD

A praying mantis's favorite foods are small insects, like grasshoppers and beetles. They also eat small animals, such as lizards and frogs. And they are known to eat other praying mantises!

LIFE CYCLE

■ **YEAR-ROUND**

HABITAT & RANGE

Most praying mantises live in Asia. They prefer tropical areas. In the United States, they are more common in the warmer southern states.

BUG ABODE

Praying mantises are one of the few insects that sleep. You can tell one is dozing when it is not moving and looks like it's drooping toward the ground.

FUN FACTS

Do you know where the praying mantis gets its name? It is named for the way it holds its front legs. It looks like it's praying!

soft egg case

hardened egg case

nymph

adult

SIZE

About ½ inch long.
That's as wide as an M&M.

HONEYBEE

Apis mellifera

Honeybees are well known for the honey and beeswax they produce. But they also play an important role in our **ecosystem**. Honeybees fly from plant to plant collecting pollen and nectar from flowers. As they visit each new flower, some pollen from a previous flower is left behind. This is called **pollination**, and it is what allows the plant to reproduce. Bees do this for many crops, including the fruits and vegetables that we eat. Without bees, farmers would not be able to produce nearly as much food as they do.

FOOD

Honeybees eat the nectar and pollen collected from flowers. They use it to make honey. Young bees eat honey, which has a lot of vitamins and nutrients to help them grow.

LIFE CYCLE

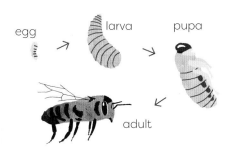

egg

larva

pupa

adult

YEAR-ROUND

HABITAT & RANGE

Honeybees live wherever there are flowering plants. Although they are not native to the United States, they now live all over the continent.

BUG ABODE

In the wild, bees live in nests. They create the nests inside empty spaces, such as tree hollows. Beekeepers use man-made hives made of wood. Inside these hives, bees build honeycomb to store food and house the eggs, **larvae**, and **pupae**.

FUN FACTS

Honeybees talk to each other by dancing. The way they move tells other bees important information, like where to find food nearby.

Each **colony** has a queen bee. She is responsible for laying eggs and can lay up to 2,000 eggs per day!

DAMSELFLY

suborder Zygoptera

Like its cousin the dragonfly, damselflies are one of the oldest groups of insects. They were here before dinosaurs! They have long, thin bodies, short **antennae**, and large eyes set far apart. The males are more colorful than the females, often showing off blue, green, red, or yellow bodies. Although they have two pairs of see-through wings, they are not great at flying. They can be slow and awkward in the air.

FOOD

Damselflies are considered useful, because they eat harmful insects, like mosquitoes. They also eat flies and moths. Some eat caterpillars and beetles. They catch **prey** in midair, grabbing insects with their hairy back legs.

LIFE CYCLE

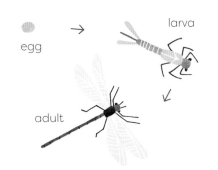

egg

larva

adult

■ **YEAR-ROUND**

HABITAT & RANGE

Damselflies live all over the world. They live near water, as they need it to reproduce.

BUG ABODE

Damselfly **nymphs** live underwater. They crawl along the bottoms of lakes, streams, and rivers looking for food. When they become adults, they leave their underwater **habitat** and stay on land. But they stay close to water where they can find a mate and reproduce.

FUN FACTS

To tell the difference between a damselfly and a dragonfly, take a look at the wings. A damselfly keeps its wings tucked in when at rest. The dragonfly keeps its wings fanned out.

SIZE

About ½ inch long.
That's as wide as a game dice.

JAPANESE BEETLE

Popillia japonica

Don't be fooled by the Japanese beetle's good looks. Its bright green and copper shell is colorful and pretty, but you don't want to see one in your yard. That's because the Japanese beetle is a pest. They feed on many types of plants, destroying them. You'll know you have Japanese beetles if your plant leaves look like skeletons of their original form.

FOOD

A Japanese beetle will eat any of about 300 different types of plants. It loves the sweet fruit from apples, plums, and peaches. It also prefers certain trees, like the Japanese maple, birch, and pin oak trees. Roses are another favorite—they love to munch on the petals.

LIFE CYCLE

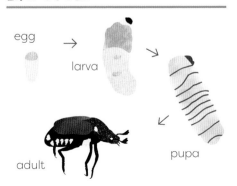

egg → larva

pupa

adult

YEAR-ROUND

HABITAT & RANGE

The first Japanese beetles in North America were spotted in New Jersey around 1916. Since then, they have spread widely. They are now in the entire eastern half of the United States.

BUG ABODE

They do well in many different climates and **habitats**. They can live anywhere there are plants for them to eat.

FUN FACTS

The Japanese beetle is named for the bug's native land, Japan. It is believed that Japanese beetle grubs hitched a ride in the soil of plants that were sent over to the United States.

SIZE

About 3 inches long.
That's as long as half of
a hot dog.

WALKING STICK

order Phasmida

The walking stick, or stick bug, is the name given to many species of brown and green sticklike insects. These bugs are experts at staying still and pretending to be sticks and twigs. And they do a good job of it! In a woodland setting, it is very difficult to spot a walking stick. This skill keeps the bug safe from predators. And they have many **predators**, such as rodents, birds, spiders, monkeys, and bats.

FOOD

Walking sticks are **herbivores**. That means they only eat plants. Leaves are a walking stick's main source of food.

LIFE CYCLE

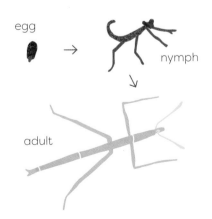

egg

nymph

adult

YEAR-ROUND

HABITAT & RANGE

Walking sticks are found in most parts of the United States.

BUG ABODE

They like tropical climates but can also live in mild climates. They are **nocturnal** and spend the daytime hiding. They don't fall asleep, but they do use this time to rest and save up their energy for nighttime when they look for food.

FUN FACTS

If a walking stick loses a leg or **antenna**, it's no big deal. It will grow back!

One species of walking stick grows to almost 2 feet in length.

Only 1 in 1,000 walking sticks are male.

Wingspan: About 2 inches.
That's about the size of two
quarters.

TIGER MOTH

family Arctiidae

There are about 11,000 species of tiger moths in the world. Many of them are medium-sized, with bold markings on their wings. They all have thin, hairlike **antennae**. You may already be familiar with one species, the Isabella tiger moth (*Pyrrharctia isabella*). It is one of the most common insects in North America. Its wings are bright yellow with black spots.

FOOD

Tiger moths drink nectar from flowers. The **larvae** of the tiger moth enjoy munching on many different types of grass, shrubs, trees, and garden crops.

LIFE CYCLE

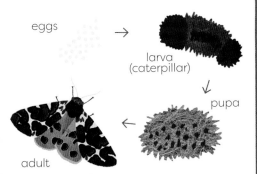

eggs →

larva (caterpillar)

pupa

adult

YEAR-ROUND

HABITAT & RANGE

They have been spotted all throughout the United States, but they will avoid the southern states in the warmer months.

BUG ABODE

They live in a variety of **habitats**, including grasslands, gardens, and woodlands. They prefer mild and cold climates.

FUN FACTS

Tiger moths' colorful wings trick **predators** into thinking they are poisonous. Their bright colors help to keep them safe.

The larvae of tiger moths are called woolly bears. Read more about them on page 81!

23

Wingspan: About 3½ inches. That's as long as a popsicle stick.

BLACK SWALLOWTAIL

Papilio polyxenes

One of the most common butterflies in the United States, the black swallowtail is easy to identify. You just need to know what to look for. It has black wings and a black body. Down the outside of its wings it has two rows of yellow spots. Another telltale sign of the black swallowtail is the short line of blue spots on the bottom of the wings. They also have two orange spots with black dots inside at the bottom of the wings. These are called **eyespots**.

FOOD

Black swallowtails love to eat plants in the carrot family, such as celery, parsley, dill, and carrots, of course. They also eat nectar from the flowers of many different plants, including thistle and clover.

LIFE CYCLE

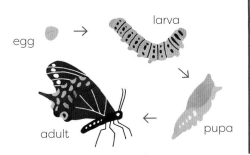

egg → larva

adult ← pupa

■ **YEAR-ROUND**

HABITAT & RANGE

You can find the black swallowtail all over the United States. They are found in almost every U.S. state except in the northwest.

BUG ABODE

This butterfly will happily live in any open area, such as fields, deserts, suburbs, and roadsides. Butterflies don't sleep, but they do rest. You may spot a butterfly hanging upside-down in a wooded area—this is likely a resting butterfly!

FUN FACTS

Eyespots are a protective feature. It draws a **predator's** attention away from the butterfly's face and body. This way, an attack is less likely to harm a bug's more important parts.

25

SIZE

About ½ inch long.
That's as long as the colorful
part of a pushpin.

EARWIG

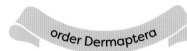

Have you ever heard the tall tale of an earwig crawling inside a human's ear and laying eggs? Although it is not likely to happen, many people still fear the earwig! They do look pretty creepy, with their set of **pincers** that stick out from their **abdomen**, but they cannot harm humans. There are about 1,800 known species of earwigs in the world. Ten of those species live in North America. They can be considered a pest in the garden for nibbling on plant leaves. However, they can also be helpful, like when they eat other insects that would do more damage.

FOOD

Earwigs eat both plants and other insects. They mainly survive on a diet of decaying plant matter.

LIFE CYCLE

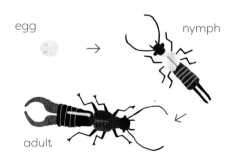

egg

nymph

adult

▦ **YEAR-ROUND**

HABITAT & RANGE

Earwigs can be found almost everywhere! In the United States, they are most common in the south and southeast.

BUG ABODE

Earwigs are **nocturnal** and stay hidden during the daytime. They find small cracks and fit into tight spaces to hide. They come out at night to find food. It is not uncommon to find earwigs in a home. They are drawn to areas where there is water, like bathrooms and kitchens.

FUN FACTS

A female earwig will visit her eggs each day, licking each one to prevent them from getting a fungus.

Some species of earwig have the ability to spit out a smelly fluid that makes them taste disgusting to **predators**.

SIZE

Wingspan: About 2 inches.
That's as long as a AA battery.

CABBAGE WHITE BUTTERFLY

Pieris rapae

The cabbage white is a small white or light yellow butterfly. They are a common sight in the spring through early fall throughout most of the United States. You can recognize these butterflies from other white butterflies because of their unique markings. The top of their wings are tipped in black, and they also have black dots on their wings. Adults are considered helpful because they **pollinate** plants as they feed. The caterpillars, on the other hand, are considered a pest. They destroy the plants they eat.

FOOD

Adults drink nectar from flowers. Caterpillars snack on the leaves of cabbage, broccoli, and other plants in the mustard family.

LIFE CYCLE

YEAR-ROUND

HABITAT & RANGE

Cabbage whites are common throughout the world. They have been spotted in every state in the United States.

BUG ABODE

This butterfly lives in many different types of open spaces, like in fields, parks, or backyards. As long as there are plants for the female butterfly to lay eggs, the cabbage white will make their home.

FUN FACTS

It's easy to tell a male cabbage white from a female. The males have just one spot on each wing and the females have two.

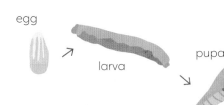

egg

larva

pupa

adult

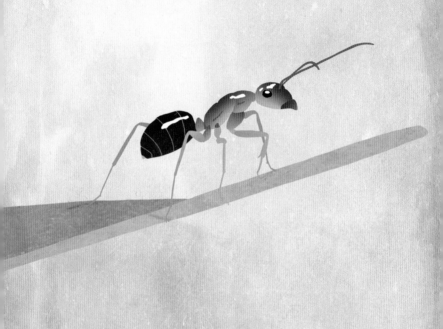

SIZE

Less than ¼ inch in length.
That's about as wide as a
pencil eraser.

ANT

family Formicidae

Ants may be tiny, but don't be fooled by their size. They are very smart and strong! There are over 10,000 species of ants throughout the world. Ants are social animals and work together in **colonies**. They are mostly black and dark brown, but some are red or yellow.

FOOD

Ants are known to eat both plant and animal matter. Some species feed on the sap from plants and fruits. Others eat insect eggs or **larvae**. Ants are known for being drawn to sweet foods, but most ants will eat almost anything!

LIFE CYCLE

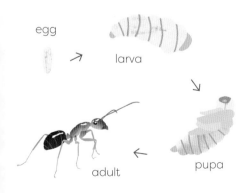

egg

larva

pupa

adult

■ **YEAR-ROUND**

HABITAT & RANGE

There are ant species all over the world, except in Greenland where it is too cold.

BUG ABODE

Most ant species live and work together in underground nests. Each ant plays a special role. There is usually one female that lays eggs. This is the queen. The males mate with the queen (and usually die after mating!). The worker ants, which are usually female, do the work of cleaning, building, finding food, and caring for the young.

FUN FACTS

Most ants are harmless to humans, but some, like the fire ant, will bite or sting if it thinks it's being attacked.

In some species, the males and the queen both have wings. They use them to mate in the air!

About 5 inches long.
That's as long as a dollar bill.

HICKORY HORNED DEVIL

caterpillar of *Citheronia regalis*

HABITAT & RANGE

The hickory horned devil is found in forests in the eastern part of the United States. They are more common in the south.

BUG ABODE

The hickory horned devil is **nocturnal**. It lives in trees until it grows to its full size. At that point, it will drop to the soil to look for a place to **pupate.** Hickory horned devils dig down in the ground and spend the winter in their **pupa**. At the beginning of the following summer, they emerge as regal moths!

If you come upon a hickory horned devil in your backyard, you might be tempted to run away as fast as you can! Based on its looks, it makes sense you might think they were very dangerous creatures. First, they are big, about the size of a large hot dog. Second, their blue-green bodies are covered in what looks like small black spikes. Worst of all, they have red and black horns on their head. Despite its fearsome appearance, this caterpillar is totally harmless to humans!

FOOD

While growing to its full size, the caterpillar lives in trees and eats leaves. Persimmon, walnut, and sumac trees are among the many types that are suitable to a hickory horned devil.

FUN FACTS

Before it forms the pupa, a hickory horned devil will shrink to about half its length and become a turquoise color!

LIFE CYCLE

eggs

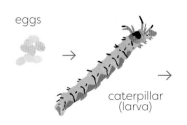

caterpillar
(larva)

pupa

adult

33

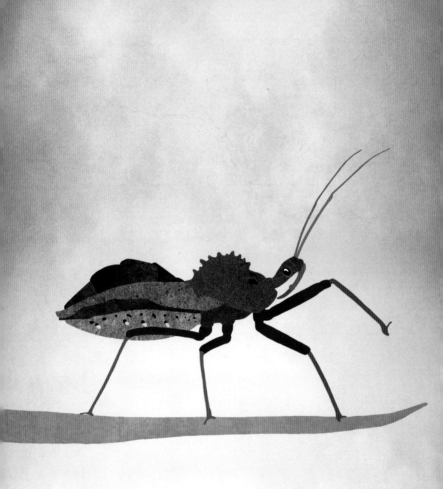

About 1 inch long.
That's about the size of two
Skittles.

WHEEL BUG

Arilus cristatus

HABITAT & RANGE

Wheel bugs are most common in the southern U.S. states, especially in the summer months.

BUG ABODE

You are not likely to see a wheel bug, as they are great at staying hidden in gardens, fields, and forests.

FUN FACTS

The eggs of the wheel bug have an unusual honeycomb-like appearance. The **nymphs** hatch directly from the eggs and go through five **molts** before becoming adults.

The wheel bug (or assassin bug as it's sometimes called) is a dull brown or gray insect. It has a very unusual feature on its back—a crest with a gear or wheel shape on top. The wheel bug is the only insect with this crest, making it an easy bug to identify. If you come across one in your yard, the best thing to do is observe it from a distance. Wheel bugs have been known to sting. And their sting is painful!

FOOD

Wheel bugs eat a variety of small insects, such as beetles, caterpillars, and moths. They are helpful in a garden, as they eat pests that destroy plants.

LIFE CYCLE

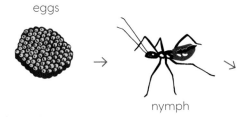

eggs

nymph

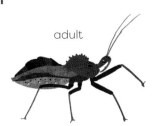

adult

SIZE

Up to 3 inches long.
They can be as small as a pea
or as long as a crayon.

CENTIPEDE

class Chilopoda

There are many species of centipede. They are all known for having many pairs of legs—between 14 and 177 pairs! The centipede you are most likely to be familiar with is called *Scutigera coleoptrata*, or the house centipede. It is the only centipede that is known to live in homes. It is about an inch long with a short, striped body and 15 pairs of long legs. It can move fast and will quickly run from danger. It can even climb walls with ease. All centipedes have the ability to sting, but a house centipede's sting can't harm you.

HABITAT & RANGE

Centipedes are found throughout the world. They have also been spotted in almost all parts of the United States.

FOOD

Centipedes are **carnivores**, or meat-eaters. They dine on spiders, moths, earthworms, and pretty much any other soft-bodied insect.

BUG ABODE

Centipedes can live in a variety of **habitats**, such as dry deserts, warm tropical areas, and near water. They are **nocturnal**. While you're sleeping, they come out to find food. During the day, they stay hidden in moist areas, like under rocks or logs.

LIFE CYCLE

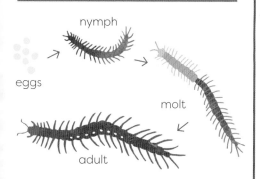

nymph

eggs

molt

adult

FUN FACTS

Some of the largest centipedes can be found in the American tropics. *Scolopendra gigantea* grows to about 11 inches in length. If you see one, stay away! They can inflict a serious bite.

37

SIZE

About 4 inches long.
That's about the length of two baseballs.

GARDEN SLUG

Arion hortensis

Slug is a general term for a soft-bodied animal in the class Gastropoda. This class includes snails and slugs from both land and sea. *Arion hortensis*, also called the garden slug, is the slug you are most likely to see in your yard. They are gray, brown, or a dull orange color. They have soft, slimy bodies that vary in size from 1 to 4 inches long. They leave a trail of slime wherever they go!

FOOD

They will eat a variety of plant matter, including roots, leaves, fruits, and vegetables. They prefer to eat the tender leaves of young plants. For this reason, they are treated as pests in a garden.

LIFE CYCLE

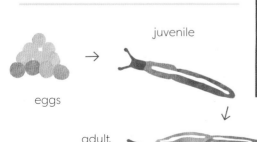

eggs

juvenile

adult

▨ **YEAR-ROUND**

HABITAT & RANGE

Garden slugs are found throughout the world and in various regions across the United States.

BUG ABODE

Garden slugs hide in dark, damp places during the day. They can be hard to see, in part because they **camouflage** with the soil. They need to be in a wet or damp environment to stay alive. Their bodies are mostly made of water and they can dry out and die without it.

FUN FACTS

The garden slug has two pairs of tentacles on its head. One set helps with sight. The other set helps with smell.

Slugs are just snails with no shell!

About 1 inch long.
That's about as long as the
head of your toothbrush.

CRICKET

family Gryllidae

Crickets are known throughout the world for their ability to jump, their musical chirps, and their long **antennae.** Some crickets have wings and can fly, while others rely on jumping to get away from danger. Crickets are often confused with grasshoppers—and for good reason. They look very much alike, although grasshoppers are usually longer and more colorful.

FOOD

Crickets eat both plant and animal matter. Depending on the species, they may prefer some foods to others. In the wild, they eat a wide variety of foods, including leaves, grains, insect **larvae**, flowers, fruits, and vegetables.

LIFE CYCLE

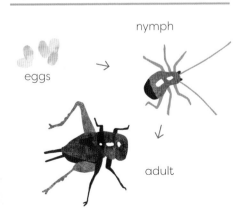

eggs

nymph

adult

YEAR-ROUND

HABITAT & RANGE

Crickets live all over the United States.

BUG ABODE

Crickets live in almost every **habitat**. They are found in forests, grasslands, marshes, beaches, roadsides, and even inside your house! They are **nocturnal** and come out at night to find food.

FUN FACTS

There are about 2,400 different species of crickets. Crickets have become a popular food item because they are high in protein. Would you eat a cricket?

About 2 inches long.
That's about as long as a tube
of Chapstick.

STAG BEETLE

The stag beetle, also known as the pinching bug, is a type of beetle found all over the world. It is usually dark brown or black and ranges in size from ⅓ inch to 1⅔ inch. It gets its name from the similarity of the stag beetle's jaw to the antlers of a stag (a male deer). Although it looks like a dangerous creature, stag beetles are not a threat to humans. The males use their jaws to fight one another.

FOOD

Stag beetle **larvae** eat rotting wood. They spend several years eating dead wood and fattening up before becoming adults. Once fully grown, they eat only tree sap.

LIFE CYCLE

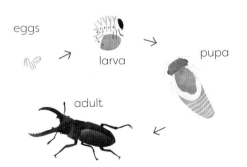

eggs

larva

pupa

adult

■ YEAR-ROUND

HABITAT & RANGE

There are over 1,000 species of stag beetle in the world. Of those, 24 are found in the United States.

BUG ABODE

Stag beetles live in forests or wooded areas with rotting logs. They need dead wood to survive. In your backyard, you might find larvae underneath a log pile or inside an old tree stump. Adult stag beetles stay hidden underground, but are they known to be drawn to light at night.

FUN FACTS

Although the larvae of the stag beetle live for several years, adults live only a few weeks.

The giraffe stag beetle is the largest stag beetle in the world. It can grow to almost 5 inches in length! Luckily, they are found only in southeast Asia.

43

SIZE

Up to 4 inches long.
That's about as long as a
green bean.

DRAGONFLY

family Anisoptera

Dragonflies are a familiar sight in the summer. They are colorful and have thin bodies, two sets of wings, and giant eyes that almost touch. In the air, they zip around like helicopters. They can even hover in midair! They are related to damselflies, but dragonflies are larger, with a length of over 2 inches.

FOOD

Dragonflies are beneficial insects. They mainly eat mosquitoes, flies, and other flying insects. They control the population of pests.

LIFE CYCLE

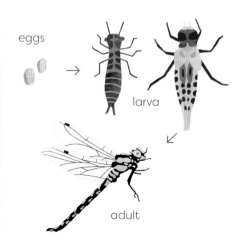

eggs

larva

adult

YEAR-ROUND

HABITAT & RANGE

Dragonflies live all over the world. The only landmass you will not find them on is Antarctica.

BUG ABODE

They live near freshwater and need it to survive. Adult dragonflies lay their eggs on the surface of a body of water. The eggs hatch in about seven days. The **larvae** will then spend the next few years underwater. There, they will hunt insects, mosquito larvae, and small fish.

FUN FACTS

Although dragonfly larvae live for a few years, adults live only for about a month!

SIZE

Up to 2 inches long.
That's as long as the shorter
side of a credit card.

WOLF SPIDER

family Lycosidae

The wolf spider gets its name from the ferocious way it hunts. Unlike most other spiders, it does not spin webs to catch **prey**. Instead, it follows its prey, then pounces like a wolf! Usually hairy and brown in color, the largest species of wolf spider is only about 1 inch long. Female wolf spiders carry their babies on their backs. When they sense danger, the babies hop off and scatter. When it happens, it looks like a single spider exploded into a hundred tiny ones!

FOOD

Wolf spiders mostly eat insects, such as ants, worms, and insect eggs. They are not afraid of larger insects and will go after prey that is bigger than them.

LIFE CYCLE

YEAR-ROUND

HABITAT & RANGE

Wolf spiders live all over the United States. They will live anywhere they can find insects to eat.

BUG ABODE

They can live in almost any climate. They prefer to be on the ground, where they can **camouflage** with dead plant matter. Sometimes they will dig a hole and burrow in soil. Other times they will make their home beneath a rock or log.

FUN FACTS

Wolf spiders have eight eyes. They have excellent vision!

egg sack

→ →

spiderlings

adult

SIZE

Wingspan: Up to 5 inches. That's about the length of a harmonica.

MONARCH BUTTERFLY

Danaus plexippus

The monarch butterfly, with its bright orange and black wings, is easy to identify. With an average 4-inch wingspan, these beauties are known for their annual **migration**. Like birds, they head south for the winter. They have been traveling great distances every fall for thousands of years!

FOOD

The eggs of the monarch butterfly are laid on milkweed leaves. When the **larvae** hatch, they feed on those leaves. Milkweed makes the adults toxic to a **predator** that dares to eat one. Adults eat only nectar from flowers.

LIFE CYCLE

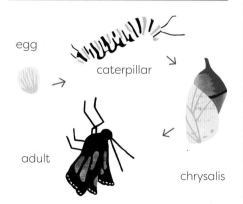

egg

caterpillar

adult

chrysalis

■ YEAR-ROUND

HABITAT & RANGE

You can find these butterflies all over the United States. They have also been spotted in Australia and India.

BUG ABODE

In the United States, monarch butterflies travel a great distance every fall. They fly as far as 2,000 miles, to California or Mexico. There, they live in trees, sometimes returning to the same tree that its ancestors once lived in!

FUN FACTS

You would need a microscope to see it, but a monarch's wings are covered in tiny, colorful scales.

49

Less than ¼ inch in length.
That's about as wide as the
fingernail on your pinkie finger.

WEEVIL

family Curculionidae

Weevils are a type of beetle with a very unusual feature. They have a long, thin snout that sticks out from the middle of its face. They use this straw-like part to eat and also to lay eggs. Their **antennae** stick out from the sides of their snout and act as feelers, helping the weevil to find food and get around. Brown in color, some weevils have wings and some do not. They can be harmful to plants and crops. And they can also do damage to your pantry! Weevils can make their way into food products like flour, cereal, grains, and beans.

FOOD

There are many species of weevil—more than 60,000 worldwide. Different species will eat different foods, but almost all eat only plants. Both the **larvae** and adults can do a lot of damage to the plants they eat.

LIFE CYCLE

YEAR-ROUND

HABITAT & RANGE

With 40,000 different kinds of weevils worldwide, weevils are everywhere except the coldest of climates!

BUG ABODE

Weevils can live in a variety of **habitats**. Most weevils are found in fields, gardens, and orchards.

FUN FACTS

Weevils are also known as snout beetles.

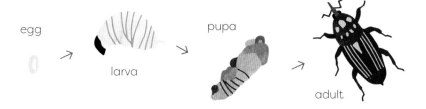

egg → larva → pupa → adult

EASTERN YELLOW JACKET

Vespula maculifrons

The eastern yellow jacket is one of many species of wasp found in the United States. Very common in the east, they are often mistaken for bees. Similar in size and coloring to bees, they also are social animals that live in **colonies**. Unlike bees, yellow jackets mostly build their nests underground. Their sting is also more painful, and a single yellow jacket can sting many times.

FOOD

Yellow jackets eat a variety of foods. They eat other insects, such as flies, bees, and caterpillars. They also eat sweet foods, like fruit and sap. In late summer and fall it is not uncommon to see yellow jackets eating sweets and soda left over from picnics.

LIFE CYCLE

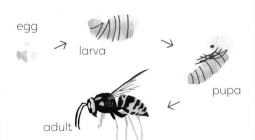

egg

larva

pupa

adult

YEAR-ROUND

HABITAT & RANGE

The eastern yellow jacket lives throughout the eastern United States. It can live in many types of **habitats**.

BUG ABODE

In the spring, a queen will begin a new colony by raising a group of workers. Those workers will then build the hive. Usually about 2 inches below the soil, the nests are made from a paperlike material. They make this material by chewing on wood and letting it mix with their saliva.

FUN FACTS

Yellow jackets and bees can be hard to tell apart. Here's a simple trick: If it has a very thin waist, you're looking at a yellow jacket. Bees are more plump around the middle.

Up to 10 inches long.
That's as long as three crayons.

MILLIPEDE

class Diplopoda

Millipedes have long, thin, wormlike bodies and many legs. Most millipedes have about 300 legs and are less than an inch long. Some grow to over 5 inches in length. The giant African millipede grows to over 11 inches in length! Almost all millipedes have a hard outer covering that acts like armor. When they sense danger, they curl into a ball to protect their soft undersides. They also have the ability to release a toxic chemical that sends **predators** away. It's not strong enough to hurt a human, but it can give you a rash. So think twice before trying to pick one up!

FOOD

Millipedes move slowly through damp dirt eating through dead wood, old leaves, and dead insects. If the soil dries out, they may also eat through the stems, roots, and leaves of live plants.

LIFE CYCLE

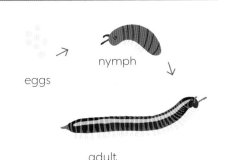

eggs

nymph

adult

■ **YEAR-ROUND**

HABITAT & RANGE

There are about 12,000 species of millipede throughout the world. The only place they don't live is Antarctica.

BUG ABODE

Millipedes live in soil. They are **nocturnal** and wait until night to look for food. During the day, they hide under garden scraps, such as leaves and logs.

FUN FACTS

Unlike centipedes, millipedes don't bite. Their mouths are only strong enough to eat soft, dying plant matter.

Would you ever want a pet millipede? If cared for properly, they can live up to 11 years!

SIZE

About ½ inch long.
That's as long as a peanut.

SIX-SPOTTED TIGER BEETLE

Cicindela sexguttata

■ **YEAR-ROUND**

Unlike other types of tiger beetle, the six-spotted tiger beetle is a bright metallic green with spots on its back. It has long legs that help it run fast and a white face with **pincers** on the sides of its mouth. It is known for hunting like tigers. It sits patiently, **camouflaged** with plants, and waits. Being very still until the time is right, it quickly pounces and catches its **prey** by surprise.

HABITAT & RANGE

Cicindela sexguttata is mainly found in the eastern United States. They can be found in wooded areas, on forest paths, and in fields near forests.

FOOD

It mainly eats other types of bugs, including ants, flies, and spiders.

BUG ABODE

The six-spotted tiger beetle needs sandy soil to live. Eggs are laid in the soil, and the **larvae** live in the ground, tunneling to the surface to eat.

LIFE CYCLE

FUN FACTS

Not all six-spotted tiger beetles have six spots! Some have fewer than six, and some have none at all.

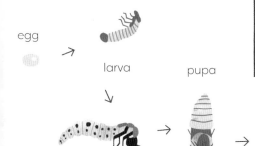

egg

larva

pupa

adult

57

SIZE

Wingspan: 4 inches.
That's as wide as a grapefruit.

LUNA MOTH

Actias luna

The luna moth is a large, light green moth seen in the spring and early summer. It is one of the largest types of moths. At the bottom of its wings, it has two long tails that hang down like streamers. Four round spots on its wings, called **eyespots**, help keep the luna moth safe from **predators**.

FOOD

Luna moth caterpillars live and munch on the leaves of a variety of plants. They like sumac, persimmon, and sweetgum, among others.

LIFE CYCLE

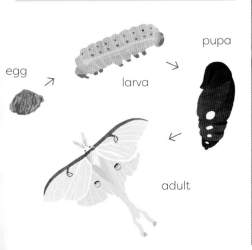

egg

larva

pupa

adult

YEAR-ROUND

HABITAT & RANGE

Luna moths can be found in the eastern half of the United States.

BUG ABODE

The luna moth lives in forested areas where there are plants for the luna moth **larvae** to eat. It sleeps during the day. At night, it looks for a mate.

FUN FACTS

Adult luna moths don't have a mouth or stomach to digest food. That's because they don't need them—they live only for a week!

About 1½ inches long.
That's as wide as a golf ball.

HORNET

genus Vespa

Hornets are a type of wasp. Often confused with yellow jackets, they are social animals that live in hives. Hornets, however, are much larger than yellow jackets. Some species are larger than 2 inches long! They have a painful sting but don't use it unless they need to protect the hive. Each **colony** has one queen that lays eggs. She will mostly produce female hornets, which become workers. They will feed the young, build the hive, hunt for food, and protect the colony.

FOOD

Hornets and their **larvae** eat other insects, such as flies and bees. They also eat tree sap.

LIFE CYCLE

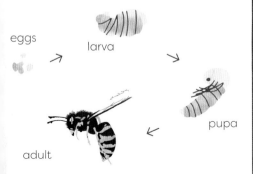

eggs

larva

pupa

adult

HABITAT & RANGE

European hornets are the only hornet species in the United States. Other species live in Asia, Europe, and Africa.

BUG ABODE

A new queen will **hibernate** through the winter and find a place to build a new hive in spring. She will form a papery material by chewing on wood. She will then use it to start to build the hive. Once she has workers to help, they will take over the work of building and maintaining the hive.

FUN FACTS

A queen will create very few male hornets. Their only purpose is to mate with the queen. Once their job is complete, they usually die.

SIZE

About ½ inch long.
That's about as long as a
peanut.

BUMBLEBEE

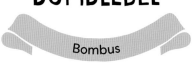

Bombus

The plump, fuzzy bumblebee stays very busy in the spring and summer. Unlike the honeybee, it does not make honey. But it has an important job: Bumblebees are **pollinators**. As they buzz from flower to flower, they move pollen from the male parts of a flower to the female parts. This helps plants to reproduce. We need plants to reproduce so that we grow enough food for humans to eat.

FOOD

Bumblebees eat nectar and pollen from flowers. If you want to help bumblebees, you can grow flowers!

LIFE CYCLE

queen overwintering

eggs

queen foraging

YEAR-ROUND

HABITAT & RANGE

Different bumblebee species are seen all over the United States. They are more common in areas with mild temperatures.

BUG ABODE

Bumblebees often build nests underground, where it is warmer than above the ground. They may take over an old bird or mouse nest. Inside, the queen lays eggs. The female workers tend to the young, gather food, and keep the nest tidy. Males, or **drones**, are born at the end of the summer. They mate with the queen.

FUN FACTS

Unlike honeybees, which can sting only once, bumblebees can sting many times.

After a queen lays eggs, she sits on them to keep them warm. She vibrates her wings to create heat. 63

SIZE

About 4 inches long.
That's as long as a toilet
paper roll.

TOMATO HORNWORM

Manduca quinquemaculata

☐ **YEAR-ROUND**

If you've ever grown tomatoes, you might be familiar with the tomato hornworm. It's a large, green caterpillar that feeds on and destroys tomato plants. Growing up to 5 inches in length, they can be quite a shock if they surprise you in your garden! You can recognize the tomato hornworm by the v-shaped stripes on its body. It also has a sharp-looking black horn on its rear. These caterpillars may look scary, but they can't hurt you.

FOOD

It eats all parts of the tomato plant. If you are dealing with a tomato hornworm infestation, the first thing you'll notice is that the leaves at the top of the plant have been chewed. It also eats eggplant, pepper, and potato plants.

LIFE CYCLE

HABITAT & RANGE

The tomato hornworm is seen all over the United States.

BUG ABODE

In late spring, adult five-spotted hawkmoths lay eggs on plant leaves. Tomato hornworms are the **larval** stage of this bug. They will grow for about three to four weeks before dropping down to the soil to **pupate**.

FUN FACTS

Chickens love to eat tomato hornworms!

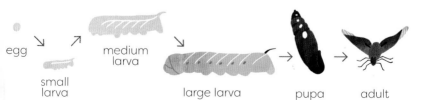

egg   small larva   medium larva   large larva   pupa   adult

SIZE

About 1 inch long.
That's as long as a hair clip.

CICADA

Cicadoidea

The cicada is an insect known for its unusual life cycle. Some species show up summer after summer. Other species will disappear for years, then come back in full force for one summer, only to disappear again. They have wide heads with big eyes and wings that are see-through. Cicadas are known for their loud buzzing and clicking noises. When there are many cicadas nearby, the sound can be as loud as a rock concert!

FOOD

They drink the sap from tree roots, branches, and twigs.

LIFE CYCLE

HABITAT & RANGE

Cicadas live all over the United States. They prefer warm summers and areas with soil that isn't too wet.

BUG ABODE

Cicadas spend most of their lives underground. As **nymphs**, they live in the soil and suck the sap from plant roots. They stay there for years before spending their short adult lives above ground. They usually live in the trees just above where they spent their younger years.

FUN FACTS

Over 1.5 million cicadas can crowd an area of just 1 acre.

There are a few cicada species that emerge only every 17 years!

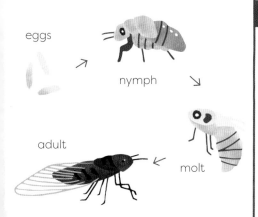

eggs

nymph

adult

molt

SIZE

About 1 inch long.
That's as long as an adult's
thumb from the knuckle.

YELLOW GARDEN SPIDER

Argiope aurantia

The yellow garden spider can have quite a different look depending on whether it is male or female. Females (seen on the left) are large, usually about ¾ to 1 inch long, with bright yellow and black coloring. They look very dangerous! Males (seen below) are about ⅓ the size of the females, and their coloring is much less bold. No matter their gender, these spiders are actually harmless to humans.

FOOD

It **preys** on many types of insects. It mostly goes after flying insects that get stuck in its web, such as flies, bees, and dragonflies.

LIFE CYCLE

HABITAT & RANGE

They are most common in the eastern United States.

BUG ABODE

The yellow garden spider can live in a variety of **habitats**. They are often seen in backyard gardens. They look for sunny areas on plants to build their webs. They are most busy in the morning and again at nightfall.

FUN FACTS

The yellow garden spider is known for its unusual zigzag web. It's the reason it gets the nickname of the zipper spider!

eggs hatch inside egg sac

spiderlings

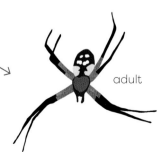

adult

SIZE

Up to 14 inches long.
That's the length of two pencils
end to end.

COMMON EARTHWORM

Lumbricus terrestris

YEAR-ROUND

HABITAT & RANGE

The common earthworm lives all over the United States.

BUG ABODE

They spend their lives underground, burrowing down in the soil as deep as 6½ feet.

FUN FACTS

Africa is home to the African giant earthworm, which averages 6 feet in length!

When you think of earthworms, what words come to mind? These slippery, slithery, wiggly, crawly creatures might not seem very important, but they are! Earthworms play a large part in keeping soil healthy. As they crawl through the dirt, the spaces they make bring air to the soil. They eat dead stuff and their poop acts as **fertilizer**. They help to keep a healthy balance of water in the earth. We have a lot to thank earthworms for!

FOOD

Earthworms eat soil and anything that's in the soil. That includes dead leaves, bug poop, bacteria, small insects, and grass.

LIFE CYCLE

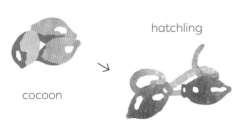

cocoon

hatchling

adult

SIZE

About 1 inch long.
That's as wide as a bottlecap.

GARDEN SNAIL

Cornu aspersum

■ **YEAR-ROUND**

A garden snail is really just a slug that carries its home on its back! Grayish-brown in color, it has a long body with four **antennae** on its head. Its shell is a hard structure that it can curl up into completely. Snails are a common sight in gardens. They are also a popular food in parts of the world! When eaten, it is called *escargot*, which is the French word for snail. Would you eat a snail?

HABITAT & RANGE

Garden snails are scattered all over the United States and in most of the world.

FOOD

They mostly munch on leaves, flowers, fruits, vegetables, and other plant parts. They will also occasionally eat dead bugs or other animal matter they come across on their travels.

BUG ABODE

Snails mostly live in gardens or wooded areas. They tend to live in areas with rich soil and places that can provide shelter.

FUN FACTS

Would you keep a snail as a pet? A pet snail that is well cared for can live to be a teenager!

LIFE CYCLE

eggs → nymph → young snail → adult

STINK BUG

family Pentatomidae

The stink bug gets its name from its unpleasant odor. It stinks! The reason for the bad smell is simple: It helps to keep stink bugs safe. Many **predators** get a whiff of a stink bug and say "no thank you!" Stink bugs are usually brown or green, but they sometimes have a bit of red. Their bodies have a shield shape. Known for being pests, they destroy crops when they use their **mouthparts** to feed on plants.

FOOD

Stink bugs feast on all sorts of plants. They use their mouthparts to pierce the plant, then inject a liquid that starts the process of digestion. Then they suck up the plant's juices. Yuck!

LIFE CYCLE

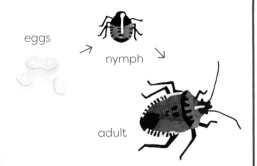

eggs

nymph

adult

■ **YEAR-ROUND**

HABITAT & RANGE

They are very widespread and their range keeps growing. Native to Asia, it is believed they first came to the United States by hitching a ride in a shipping container!

BUG ABODE

You can find stink bugs wherever there are crops to feed on. They are also commonly found in homes. They find their way in looking for warmth in the cooler months.

FUN FACTS

In Mexico and some southeast Asian countries, stink bugs are included in some cuisines. Their odor is described as "spicy."

Stink bugs are known to invade a house in large numbers. A scientist in Maryland counted over 26,000 in his home in a six-month period!

SIZE

Less that ¼ inch.
About the size of an apple seed.

TICK

suborder Ixodida

Ticks may be tiny in size, but they can cause a great deal of harm. These eight-legged bugs are usually black, brown, or reddish-brown, but sometimes they are yellow or gray in color. They most often live in wooded areas, spending much of their time waiting for a mammal to climb onto. They then use special **mouthparts** to suck blood from their host. Ticks can carry bacteria that cause serious diseases, such as Lyme disease and Rocky Mountain spotted fever.

FOOD

Ticks drink blood from mammals. Young **larvae** and **nymphs** will usually feed on small animals, such as mice. Adult ticks will usually feed on larger animals, such as horses and deer, and even humans.

LIFE CYCLE

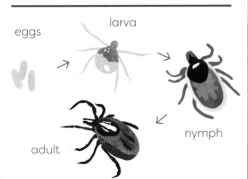

eggs

larva

nymph

adult

■ **YEAR-ROUND**

HABITAT & RANGE

Ticks are found all over the United States. Scientists are finding that many tick species are spreading every year.

BUG ABODE

Most kinds of ticks live in fields and woods. The larvae, nymphs, and adults all pose a danger to other animals. An adult tick can wait up to three years to find a host.

FUN FACTS

Many ticks don't have eyes. They use their sense of smell and the vibrations from movement to find a host.

Some tick bites can cause a person to become allergic to eating meat! The allergy can cause serious, life-threatening symptoms.

Less than ¼ inch.
That's smaller than a staple.

LADYBUG

family Coccinellidae

Colorful, cute, and totally harmless, ladybugs are thought to be a sign of good luck. They have colorful, oval-shaped bodies and black heads. Most commonly, they are red with black spots, but some are orange, yellow, brown, or black. They are active in spring, summer, and fall. In the winter, they **hibernate** in **colonies**, sometimes with thousands of other ladybugs.

FOOD

They eat other insects and insect eggs. Farmers sometimes buy ladybugs to help keep unwanted pests under control.

LIFE CYCLE

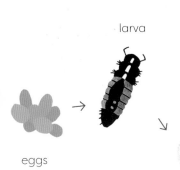

larva

eggs

pupa

adult

YEAR-ROUND

HABITAT & RANGE

Ladybugs live almost everywhere! They avoid places with the coldest temperatures but are found all over the rest of the world.

BUG ABODE

Ladybugs can live in many different **habitats**. They are seen in cities, suburbs, forests, and near rivers.

FUN FACTS

The ladybug's bright color is a warning to **predators**. It lets them know that ladybugs do not taste good.

A single ladybug can eat up to 5,000 insects in its life!

SIZE

About ½ inch long.
That's as long as a kidney
bean.

WOOLLY BEAR

caterpillar of *Pyrrharctia isabella*

Woolly bears are adorable fuzzy caterpillars with black and brown stripes. They are the **larvae** of the tiger moth! After hatching from an egg, they **molt** six times before reaching their full size. Usually seen in the fall, they go on to spend the winter **hibernating**. Many people believe that the longer the black bands on a woolly bear, the longer and snowier the winter will be. Do you think the woolly bear's stripes can predict the weather?

FOOD

They eat many different types of grass, shrubs, trees, and garden crops.

LIFE CYCLE

■ **YEAR-ROUND**

HABITAT & RANGE

Woolly bears are found in the same places as the tiger moth, of course! They live in most parts of the United States.

BUG ABODE

Woolly bears can live in many different **habitats**. They are active in the spring, summer, and fall. During the winter, they hibernate. They can withstand freezing cold temperatures.

FUN FACTS

Woolly bears curl into a ball and play dead when they sense danger.

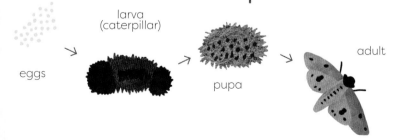

eggs → larva (caterpillar) → pupa → adult

Up to 2½ inches long.
That's about as wide as a
baseball.

KATYDID

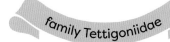

family Tettigoniidae

■ **YEAR-ROUND**

Katydids are often confused with crickets and grasshoppers. They all show up in shades of green. And they all have straight wings that they hold close to their bodies. But there are a lot of differences too. Unlike grasshoppers, katydids are **nocturnal**. And unlike crickets, katydids keep their legs close to their bodies, instead of being spread out. You can identify a katydid by the sound and timing of its call. It makes a very loud raspy chirp, and they make it at night. You are more likely to hear a katydid than see one!

HABITAT & RANGE

You can find katydids all over the United States. However, they are most common in tropical areas.

BUG ABODE

Katydids can survive in many different climates. They live in areas with lots of plants. They need plants for food and also to **camouflage**.

FOOD

Katydids eat lots of leaves. They also eat small insects, fruit, and grass.

FUN FACTS

Katydids use their legs to hear!

Most katydids are brown, but about 1 in 500 are bright pink!

LIFE CYCLE

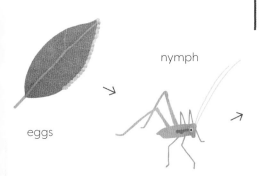

eggs

nymph

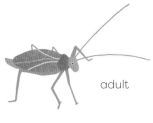

adult

SIZE

About ½ inch long.
That's about as wide as a
blueberry.

PILL BUG

Armadillidium vulgare

The pill bug has a unique look. Covered in segments that look like armor, it resembles the armadillo (but much smaller, of course!). It is dark gray in color. Sometimes known as a roly-poly, the pill bug gets its name from the shape it makes when it senses danger. To protect itself, it curls up into a tight pill-shaped ball. You're more likely to see them after it has rained, so keep an eye out after the next storm!

FOOD

The pill bug mostly eats decaying plant matter. This helps keep the soil healthy.

LIFE CYCLE

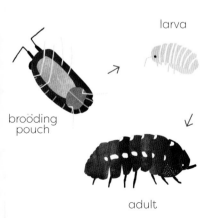

larva

brooding pouch

adult

YEAR-ROUND

HABITAT & RANGE

Pill bugs live all over the United States. They thrive in areas with mild temperatures. They cannot survive in areas that are very warm or dry.

BUG ABODE

Pill bugs need water to breathe, so they must live in damp environments. They prefer to hide in dark, wet areas during the day, then come out at night.

FUN FACTS

What do pill bugs have in common with lobsters, shrimp, and crabs? They all use **gills** to breathe. For this reason, pill bugs must stay damp. Without moisture, they can't breathe.

The female pill bug does not lay her eggs. Instead, she carries them inside her **brooding pouch**. This is like a pocket on the underside of a pill bug. It keeps the eggs safe.

85

SIZE

About ½ inch long.
That's as long as a black bean.

BLUE-WINGED WASP

Scolia dubia

The blue-winged wasp gets its name from the blue shimmer of its wings. These fuzzy flying bugs have shiny black heads and two yellow spots on their **abdomen**. They are considered a beneficial insect because they eat bugs that are known to destroy plants. Although they have the ability to sting, they aren't much of a threat to humans.

FOOD

The blue-winged wasp loves to eat beetle grubs. In the summer months, the wasp will hunt them by flying low over lawns. They also eat nectar from flowers.

LIFE CYCLE

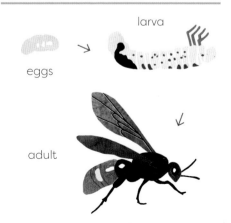

eggs

larva

adult

■ **YEAR-ROUND**

HABITAT & RANGE

They are active across most of the United States.

BUG ABODE

Blue-winged wasps are drawn to open areas with lots of flowers. In the early morning hours, you might catch a glimpse of a group of males sleeping on plant stems. It is believed that they rest in groups as a safety measure.

FUN FACTS

Females that are ready to lay eggs will sometimes find a grub to lay her egg on. When it hatches, the hungry **larva** then eats the grub!

SIZE

About 2 inches long.
That's as wide as a pool ball.

GRASSHOPPER

suborder Caelifera

There are about 18,000 different kinds of grasshoppers in the world! They range in color and size, but they are all excellent jumpers. They use their jumping skills to get away from **predators**. Grasshoppers have very strong jaws and can destroy crops by eating their way through huge quantities of plants. You definitely don't want grasshoppers in your garden.

FOOD

Most grasshoppers are **herbivores**. Their diet consists of eating grasses. A few species of grasshopper will also eat some animal matter.

LIFE CYCLE

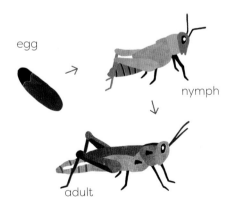

egg

nymph

adult

■ **YEAR-ROUND**

HABITAT & RANGE

Grasshoppers live all over the United States, except in freezing cold areas.

BUG ABODE

They live in a variety of climates, including deserts, mountains, and tropical forests. Some can even live in water! They are the most common in dry areas that have lots of grass and plants for them to eat.

FUN FACTS

Grasshoppers are one of the oldest insects. Fossils have been found that date back 250 million years!

If a grasshopper senses danger, it may puke up smelly vomit to keep a predator away.

Grasshoppers are a popular snack food in some parts of the world.

MY BUG LOG

Here you can keep track of all the bugs you have spotted. In the Notes column, add details about the bug's appearance or behavior.

NAME OF BUG	DATE	LOCATION	NOTES

NAME OF BUG	DATE	LOCATION	NOTES

CONSERVATION

Bugs play an important role in our world. They do the hard work of **pollinating** flowering plants, making it possible for us to grow the food we eat. Bugs are also the main source of food for other animals, such as birds, reptiles, and fish. They also keep our soil clean and healthy by eating decaying matter. Without bugs, we would be in trouble.

Here are a few ways you can help protect bugs:

⇀ Let part of your garden grow wild. Bugs are happier in areas that are closer to their natural **habitat**.

⇀ Plant wildflowers! Not only are they pretty to look at, they will also provide a habitat for bugs.

⇀ Talk to your parents about the use of pesticides in your yard. Many of the chemicals we use around our homes are deadly to bugs.

⇀ Consider your family's carbon footprint. Are there things you could be doing to lower it? Using reusable grocery bags, cutting back on eating meat, and recycling will all lessen your family's impact on the environment. A healthy environment can help keep bugs healthy.

The Center for Biological Diversity is an organization focused on protecting nature. They have programs for kids. You can find out more on their website (www.biologicaldiversity.org).

Talk to your friends, family, and teachers about the importance of bugs on our world. Share with them some ideas for ways they can help!

GLOSSARY

abdomen The rear section of a bug that contains the stomach and other organs used for digestion and reproduction.

antennae The parts of an insect that are used for smell or to help feel what's around.

camouflage The act of blending into surroundings to hide.

colony A group of insects living in a dwelling together.

ecosystem All of living things in an area.

eyespot A round marking on a butterfly or moth that looks like an eye.

habitat The natural home of a plant or animal.

herbivore An animal that eats only plants.

hibernate To spend time being inactive, usually in the winter.

larva The wormlike juvenile form of an insect.

migration The movement from one area to another, usually seasonally.

molt   The process of shedding skin as an insect grows.

mouthparts   The part of an insect that is used for chewing and eating.

nocturnal   Active at night.

nymph   A young insect.

pincers   The curved claws of an insect.

pollination   The act of moving pollen so that a plant can reproduce.

predator   An animal that lives by killing and eating another animal.

prey   An animal that is hunted and killed by another animal.

pupa   The cocoon inside which an insect transforms into an adult.

pupate   To become a pupa; transitioning from larva to adult insect.

First Edition
27 26 25 24 23   5 4 3 2 1

Published by Gibbs Smith
P.O. Box 667 Layton, Utah 84041
1.800.835.4993 orders
www.gibbs-smith.com

Designed by Virginia Snow and Nicole LaRue
Manufactured in China November 2022 by RR Donnelley Asia Printing Solutions.

Gibbs Smith books are printed on either recycled, 100% post-consumer waste, FSC-certified papers or on paper produced from a 100% certified sustainable forest/controlled wood source.

Library of Congress Control Number: 2022943889
ISBN: 978-1-4236-6265-5

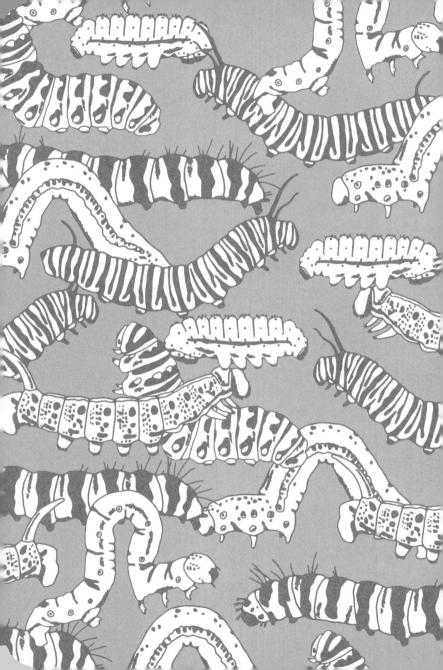